From Child*HOOD* To Man

Slipping? Falling? You. Can. Get Up!

By
Maurice Lennon

Conscious Dreams
PUBLISHING

From ChildHOOD To Man: Slipping? Falling? You. Can. Get Up

First Printed in United Kingdom 2022

Published by Conscious Dreams Publishing
www.consciousdreamspublishing.com

Edited by Elise Abram and Daniella Blechner

Typeset by Oksana Kosovan

ISBN: 978-1-915522-17-7

Dedication

FIRST, THANKS BE TO the Almighty. 'In him I live move *and have my being.*' Thanks to the ancestors: the shoulders I stand on.

Thanks to everyone who has touched my life in a positive way, especially those mentioned in this book. Thanks to my late mother Iota Deltoria Lennon Baugh, affectionately called Pat.

I would also like to say a big thank you to Denise, my Queen, for all her support, help, and encouragement. She was my inspiration for writing this book and making its publication possible. I couldn't have done it without her. Thank you so very much for everything!

This book is also dedicated to my three children, two grandchildren, and all children from Hoods, Ghettos and Endz—however termed—who survived and/or did not survive the realm of "inevitable" designed statistics.

Special thanks to my cousins Marky for all his support and to Doreen Stanley for all the love and support over the years. Thank you.

If there is anyone else who knows me and I have not mentioned you within these pages, thank you! Thank you all!!

Maya Angelou said, 'There is no greater agony than bearing an untold story inside you.'

We all have stories deserving to be heard and learned from. Experience teaches. Here is my story.

Contents

Introduction

"

Sometimes a fruit falls from a tree and rolls so far away from its roots that it's no longer of the tree. The hard fall, and long journey, bruises the fruit so much that it totally changes it. It's the same way for some of our people. This is why some can't be awakened regardless of how much truth you present to them. This journey has totally brainwashed them to such a degree that they're no longer of the original tree.

~ Malcolm X

"

I HAVE A DREAM, and I am The Dream: The Dream in search of and back to that tree Malcolm X speaks of in the above quote. One of my Dreams today, as I seek my true purpose and reason for still being alive in these times, is to write my life's story. I have always wanted to write my life's story, and throughout the course of my life's journey, a number of people have said that I should. I started to do so in 2020, and if you are holding my book in your hands, that Dream has been realised.

At the beginning of the book writing process, I found out that my (great) grandfather had dared to live and follow his Dreams. Unbeknownst to me, he has been an unknown and unsung hero in my life. When I read about all he achieved in his life, it floored me. When I was younger people said I looked like him, but at the time I did not know who he was, and did not know of his great works.

Allow me to introduce him here. Here are excerpts taken from two different articles written about him and his life's achievements. The first story is written by Oluwole Osagie-Jacobs in *The Nation Nigerian News and Current Events*, 1st January, 2015, in Education, and the other is taken from *The Jamaican Gleaner*, published on 28th October, 2015 by Horace Fish. For further information, please refer to for full article.

It has been 50 years now since the death of Archdeacon Lackland Augustus Lennon, M.B.E., O.B.E., J.P. (1885-1964), the quintessential clergy sent by providence to the Akoko and the Ebira of Ondo and Kogi states to preach the gospel and introduce western education and development.

Lennon was born in Mocho, Clarendon, Jamaica, in 1885. He was a tall black Christian missionary of the Anglican Communion whose first assignment in Nigeria was teaching at the St. Andrews College, Oyo, in the second decade of the last century. In 1920, Lennon (then a reverend) was posted to Ikare-Akoko as a church superintendent with a mandate to propagate Christianity in the area.

Lennon's built churches, schools, dispensaries, postal agencies and constructed roads. He introduced modern agriculture and taught people the art of masonry and carpentry. He was a missionary not only of the word but with multiple calling (sic) for various teachings. From 1920-1951 remain his golden years...

During Nigeria's independence ceremony in 1960, he was one of the eminent personalities honoured with an invitation by the government. In 1977, the Anglican community in Ebira renamed Igbirra (Ebira) Anglican College after this illustrious son of Africa and the world. The school is now known as Lennon Memorial College, Ageva in Okene Local Government Area of Kogi State. One of the school's distinguished alumni is the journalist, playwright and politician, Dr Adinoyi Ojo Onukaba...

Jamaican Gleaner, published Wednesday, October 28, 2015 at 8:51 a.m. by Horace Fisher:

MOCHO, Clarendon, Jamaica:

In 1969, Mocho Junior Secondary School opened its doors open to 500 students and 27 staff members. Forty-five years later and several name changes, Lennon High School has emerged as one of Jamaica's finest educational institutions, providing sound education for thousands of men and women of honour.

The learning institution, which is located in the cool, serene hills of the Mocho Mountains, in marking the occasion of the milestone, paid tribute to its founder, Augustus Larkland Lennon, member of the Most Excellent Order of the British Empire, Officer of the Most Excellent Order of the British Empire, justice of the peace, and Archdeacon Emeritus of Lagos...

'What a journey it has been for Lennon High! Since opening our doors in 1969 as the then Mocho Junior Secondary School, this institution has grown by leaps and bounds from a population of 500 students to well over 1,150 today. At inception, our staff complement stood at just 27. That, too, has expanded to 88 staff members,' Dr Donald Johnson, the school's principal, said.

He added: 'Over the years, the school has been upgraded from a junior secondary to a secondary, a comprehensive high before attaining its current status as a high school where our students know that they are among a privileged cadre to attend one of Clarendon's most sought-after high schools,' Johnson asserted in his address at Monday's 45th anniversary and Founder's Day ceremony in Mocho, Clarendon.

Oftentimes, the apple does not fall too far from the tree, and when it does, it can find its way back. This Lennon legacy gene is in me, and it has guided me, however nightmarish some of my life's situations and experiences have been. I hope that, in the telling of my life's story, this oral history will uplift and inspire all those who read it, especially Black boys and men from African and Caribbean descent. It is my hope that it will uplift and help these boys and men realise their true potentials and build self- and race-confidence.

I believe that we all have an overcoming story of our own and/ or another Dream of some kind inside of us, wanting to come out. Here is my statistic-defying, confidence-realising, Tree-of-Life-finding life story...

Beating Statistics

ONE EVENING, I DECIDED TO drive through my old neighbourhood on my way to pick up a patient at Long Island University Hospital in downtown Brooklyn. I had a new job driving an ambulance, taking patients to and from dialysis. Bergen Street, Prospect Heights (Brooklyn), used to be a tough street in a tough neighbourhood. Bergen Street ran all the way through 5th Avenue, which was the headquarters for gangs in Brooklyn once upon a time. The neighbourhood had changed dramatically through something called gentrification —a good thing for some, not so much for others. The same thing is happening in London and in most major cities, where low-income renters are being pushed out of their homes through rent increases and forced to uproot their lives and livelihood in search of sustainable and affordable accommodations.

I made the left onto Bergen Street. The old neighbourhood looked like a ghost town as I drove through, complete with tumbleweeds blowing down the street like in the old cowboy movies.

I looked and saw a lone figure walking down my old block, Bergen Street, and lo and behold, to my surprise it was Louie, an old gang member from back in the day. They called him Mr Kool, but I often called him Mr Fool behind his back. He used to be the leader for the Savage Skulls Gang, who ran 5th Avenue in Brooklyn back in the day.

I shouted to him and said, 'Louie! What's up?'

He looked at me for what seemed an eternity, probably trying to assess all the names and faces of people he'd done wrong, then his eyes widened, he broke into a smile, and said, 'D—that you? How you doing? It's been a long time!' (D being short for Danny).

I said, 'Louie, where's everybody at?'

He looked me dead in the eye and said, 'D, everybody's dead or in jail and never coming home.'

I said, 'Man, it *can't be* that bad!? Where's Juan?'

He said, 'Dead.'

I said, 'Where's Chino?'

He said, 'Jail, doing fifty years.'

I said, 'Papo?'

He said, 'Dead. Everyone's gone. I'm the last one left.' He went on to say that everyone we'd known had died of AIDS, heroin, or been killed. I suddenly felt a slight sense of jubilation that I was still here; I could so easily have been amongst the statistics.

Let me take you back.

PART ONE

NATURE & NURTURE

The Roll From the Tree

FROM CHILDHOOD TO MAN, 1962–1998

CHAPTER 1

The UK JA USA Experience

I WAS BORN IN London, England, at Park Royal Hospital, Harlesden, in 1962. One of seven children, I was the only one born in England. I am the youngest, the wash belly, as they call it in Jamaica. I don't have any memories of my first two years of life spent in England, but that is where my life's story begins.

I was sent to Jamaica at a young age to take the pressure off of my momma, as it was difficult for her to work and take care of me at the same time. My father was missing in action at the time. When I was two years old, she sent me to Jamaica to live with my grandmother. My five brothers and one sister were already in Jamaica because they were born there. Most immigrant African/

West Indians in those days depended on their extended families for support 'back home,' as it's affectionately called.

My mother got married to my stepfather in 1970 when she came to Jamaica to bring us all to the USA. He remained in Jamaica for a short time, due to immigration formality, before joining the family in New York not too long afterwards.

Anyway, I was put on a plane by myself at two years old, and the story goes that when I arrived in Jamaica, no one had bothered or thought to change my nappy on the journey. I was told I arrived in Jamaica full of shit.

My grandma's place was known as Big Yard because, more often than not, there were a lot of us there. My brothers and some cousins lived there. She was the extended family that all of her children sent their kids to whilst they focused on making a living overseas. Us kids all got along well. We went to Mocho Primary School in Clarendon. We went bird hunting together, which consisted of making homemade slingshots, and we would go in search of perfectly made stones that fit into the slings. We played marbles, we argued, and we fought, but we remained mostly quite tight. Those days were the best memories of my childhood.

Later, my five brothers, me, my sister, Dawn—who we protected very much—and my stepfather, Mr Baugh, all came together in Duhaney Park, Sherlock Crescent, in Kingston, as some of us lived in different places in Jamaica. It was the first time we would all be under one roof. This was in January 1970. Things were tough financially at the time. My brother Bobby was the only one working in Patrick City, an adjoining community. In

August 1970, after what seemed like an eternity, the day finally came to leave for the USA.

After six years spent in Jamaica, it was time to leave for New York. In August 1970, we arrived at Bergen Street, Brooklyn, New York. It was me, my brother Barry, Bobby, and my sister Dawn. My other two brothers, Johnny and Dicky, came later. I must say, the pretty lights we saw from thousands of feet up over New York at night greeting our arrival didn't materialise as dawn gave way to daylight. Brooklyn and the surrounding Boroughs of New York in the seventies were war zones, complete war zones with burnt-out buildings, old cars left to rot by the roadside, and junkies making nests in them. Gangs ran wild all over the streets. Remember the movie *Gangs of New York*? It was that kind of scene.

A few of the gangs that ran around my neighbourhood were the Savage Skulls, the Puerto Rican Outlaws, and the Black Desperados. The Mau Mau were also around but farther down 5th Avenue in Sunset Park. Gangs were everywhere, and besides having to deal with the gangs, we West Indians arriving in New York in the seventies had the Yankees to deal with. That's what we called the Black Americans when they targeted and blamed us for coming to their country to steal or take their jobs and housing, which was far from the truth. Truth be told, not many Black Americans from my hood worked, depending mostly on the government's welfare program, while the West Indians did the jobs no one else wanted.

In the seventies, the USA was going through a recession, and you could see the desperation and hunger on people's faces. Going to the grocery store was a mission as you had to literally walk around with four eyes watching in case you were robbed or worse. The streets were a dangerous place. In those days, it seemed that more people than not lived in the Projects, what's known in England as the Council Estates. Brooklyn had many projects, and they were dangerous places, such as the Pink Houses, Starrett City, the Brownsville Houses, and Lafayette Gardens. I don't know why they put the 'garden' in it, as all you ever saw were bullet holes and graffiti; I never once saw a garden there. I had a good friend from there who needlessly lost his life. His name was Skip. He's just another statistic in the hood now, shot at a block party for eyeballing the wrong man.

There are more projects I didn't mention, such as the Redhook Projects, the Marlborough Projects, Wycoff, and others. I think Brooklyn has more projects than anywhere else in the Big Apple, maybe because it's the biggest borough. They call New York 'The Big Apple' because it's supposed to be **so big and sweet** that everyone wants a bite, but the jury is still out on that one.

CHAPTER 2

Outcast

IN JANUARY 1971, I STARTED at my first school, PS9, which was a massive public school at St Marks and Underhill Avenues, which wasn't far from my house. It was my zone school, which meant that everyone from my neighbourhood, which was, at the time, Prospect Heights, went there. Crown Heights was the adjoining neighbourhood, and we all went to the same schools because we shared the same zone. It was a form of a racial line/ divide between the neighbourhoods, keeping the whites on one side and the Blacks and Latinos on the other.

I started in the third grade because when I left Jamaica, I had already finished the first and second grades, so I didn't have to repeat any grades. First, let me say that, in the early 1970s, West Indians had to join forces for protection, as we were under attack by Black America. Most days, we had to run home after school with what seemed like half of the school chasing us. Such was life in the early seventies — you had to fight or flight, and most times, we were outnumbered, so the decision wasn't hard. This went on until the late seventies.

I remember when my cousins — Tony and his brother, Junior — came to New York from Jamaica; this was in 1973. They had the pet names of Bim and Bam because whenever they fought, that was the sound they made when throwing punches. Bim and Bam, just like Batman and Robin. I was happy when they came because although I had brothers, we didn't hang out because they were older. Now, I had a team.

I remember one summer's day when Tony, Junior, and I decided to go swimming at Douglass Pool on Douglass Street in Brooklyn. We had a good time in the pool, and when it was time to leave, we went to the lockers only to find that they had been broken into. Our sneakers were stolen, and we had to walk home barefoot. The next day, we went back and busted a few lockers to compensate for our losses. We later found out that a guy called King Allah stole our sneakers. He was the neighbourhood troublemaker, although there were a lot of those, and at the time, it seemed as if everyone was up to no good. That's why school was my favourite place, as it taught me, through books, how to open my imagination and use it to escape from the usual smell of stress, poverty, and desperation in the city.

English, History, and Music were some of my favourite subjects in school, but my real favourite was music class, and my favourite teacher was the music teacher. I had a schoolboy crush on her. She was kind, and she treated me nicely; not that any of them treated me badly, but she was extra nice. She sang songs, and we would follow. I behaved extra well in Miss Wong's class. All of the teachers liked me. They liked my smile and would sometimes tell my mother about her son's beautiful smile during PTA meetings. I was a kind of teacher's pet in those days, but the daily struggle to fit in and be a part of the community and society as a whole was very stressful, to say the least. It was made extra hard because I was outcast by my own community, the Black Americans.

All that said and done, there was a silver lining in my dark clouds, and her name was Charlene. She lived next door. I thought she was the prettiest girl I'd ever seen. The first day I arrived, she came over and said, 'Hi,' with a smile that could melt the sun.

I said, 'Hi,' and that was all she wrote. We often sat on the fire escape, talking until our parents called us in, or we'd hang out on the roof at night as the summers were sizzling hot, and anywhere we could escape the heat was welcome. Whenever we could, we'd turn on the fire hydrant and put a sprinkler cap on it or just use a can with the top and bottom cut off and shoot the water at each other. It was a pleasure to get wet and eat Mr Softie ice cream with her when the truck came by.

She was my first girlfriend—I believe it's called puppy love, what with us both being eight years old. So, I asked the million-dollar question: 'Do you want to be my girlfriend?'

She said, 'Yes,' and we kissed for the first time. Our first-time kiss included spittle running down our chins, but the rest is history. We were close until we got to junior high school, and then we slowly drifted apart. We remained close friends until her parents moved out of the neighbourhood, like so many other families who were concerned about the never-ending high crime rate.

I couldn't complete this story of my first puppy love with Charlene without mentioning Arlene and Pat. They were like my sisters, especially Arlene who I considered to be my little sister. We all grew up together on Bergen Street. To this day, Arlene and Pat still live in the same house. Arlene went on to marry a friend of mine and named her daughter Danielle: my namesake. I still feel honoured and blessed to have a connection with them and to still have them in my life to this date.

Seventies Brooklyn was a hard place in hard times. My mother, God rest her soul, did two jobs and was our rock. She used to tell us not to hang out in front of the house or sit on the steps as it might encourage a crowd. Anything could happen, and more times than not, it did. There was a shooting every other day. As kids on the way to school, we faced death often. Me and my friend liked to arrive at school in time for the early bird free breakfast. It wasn't that I did not get breakfast at home; I just loved my food. On occasion, we'd see the odd poor soul who had nowhere to shield from the cold trying to keep warm around a burning drum in zero degrees. Drinking Wild Irish Rose mixed with drugs, some homeless men would eventually freeze to death. After experiencing this a few times, and on the way to becoming desensitized, racing to school for the free breakfast, we didn't think twice about jumping over dead bodies. Though, for me as a child, it did continue to secretly hurt me each time I saw a homeless dead body, thinking that just hours ago this had been a living soul. Such was the deprivation and suffering in Brooklyn during these times: thick in the air.

In July 1975, I was eleven years old. It was a hot summer's day. I was getting ready for bed, just after 11 p.m, when I heard what sounded like firecrackers outside. I ran to the window and looked out to see my oldest brother holding his chest and saying to my brother Barry, 'They shot me.'

My brother Simroy and his friend had been sitting on our steps just talking when a guy walked by. My brother's friend said, 'Hello,' and it seemed like the guy didn't like that for whatever reason, and he decided to start shooting.

My brother's friend ran into the house, but my brother had been shot three times for no good reason whatsoever. The culprit was never caught, but I'm a strong believer in karma; you reap what you sow. We all pay for the harm we do, one way or another.

The ambulance took a very long time to come because of the neighbourhood, and the police had to come before or at the same time as the ambulance. I believe it has something to do with crime scenes, but in this case, it seemed the police didn't care much about another shooting in the hood.

My brother bled out and died in the Methodist Hospital in Brooklyn, where my mother worked. I was eleven years old at the time, and I didn't know how to process what had happened. I was crushed and left to deal with it—and my grief—on my own. I felt sad, angry, stressed, and confused. My brother Simroy died on 4th July on my brother Barry's birthday and Independence Day.

We all went to Jamaica for the funeral. We spent two weeks there, going to the funeral and seeing family and old friends. I wanted to stay to play in what had been the best place in my life, where I'd had the best time of my life until then, but I had to return to school.

After returning to New York from Jamaica, I felt and sensed a change in myself and my brothers. It was the realisation that there was no place for weakness if you wanted to survive in that environment. It was a dog-eat-dog environment: you either did or died.

I headed for junior high school, looking at the world through wiser, clearer, and less innocent eyes. Yes, life continued, but I missed my brother big time. I carry that loss with me to this day.

CHAPTER 3

Another Dish of Trauma

ADVERSE CHILDHOOD EXPERIENCES CONTINUED for me. Today, I know that there are names for these early experiences that happen as we go and grow through life, especially for Black people. Names like *bereavement*, *complex trauma*, *stress* and *ptsd- post traumatic stress disorder*—and the mental health vulnerabilities that comes along with it.

In 1976, when I was twelve years old, I spent a lot of time around my uncles and aunts. We were a close family. My grandmother, God rest her soul, had nine children, which gave me a lot of cousins my age to hang with, and we would always go from home to home, especially on Thanksgiving and Christmas. My Uncle Percy was a big, strong, powerful man who lived by himself, so my cousins Bim and Bam and I often went to his house for money. He was also a kind man.

My uncle decided he needed a wife, and he took off for Jamaica to find her. He went to our community in Mocho to seek out a very pretty young lady by the name of Joy, and believe me, she was a joy to look at (no pun intended). My uncle approached her family about his intentions, and they readily agreed. In those days, things were particularly hard, and it was believed that he could provide her with a better life and more opportunities, so they gave their blessing, and off she went to her new life in New York with my uncle.

Things seemed to be going well for a few years or so until, one day, he went to work and came home to find the house empty. Joy moved out while he was at work. He searched high and low to no avail. He walked the streets day and night, looking for her. This was heartbreaking for us as we had never seen him show any vulnerability. We had no knowledge of mental illnesses or what stress can do — you were just expected to take everything in stride or risk being seen as weak. I must say, his situation was nothing new. A lot of women and men entered a marriage, got to the USA, and ran off, as getting to the USA was the goal. It was a bitter pill to swallow, and not everyone could handle the emotional and psychological aspects of being abandoned.

A few weeks after Joy had left, my brothers and I were in our room playing music, and the door burst open. My uncle was wild-eyed and frothing in a rage, and he began smashing everything in the room, including the turntable, as it was called in those days.

My brothers tried to subdue him, but it was useless as he was too strong. My grandfather called him The Bull for that same reason.

We later learned that he believed my brothers had somehow been intimate with his wife before she'd run off, which was the start of his distorted thinking. It grew into a snowball and gathered momentum as he spiralled out of control.

The police were called, and he was taken away for psychiatric evaluation. This was the beginning of his mental breakdown. He was later diagnosed as being in the early stages of schizophrenia and put on medication. Although my uncle was a strong man physically, he didn't cope too well mentally, and not so long after being released he had another breakdown.

My mother, my stepfather, and I slept on the ground floor of our house while my brothers slept upstairs. One summer night, while everyone was asleep, my uncle managed to open the front window and come into our apartment. He picked up a pair of scissors and went to my mother's room, where he tried to stab my stepfather. My stepfather was stabbed in his hand, trying to defend himself, and my mother was stabbed trying to stop him. Thankfully, it wasn't serious.

I woke up to screams and shouts and looked up to see my uncle standing over me with a bloody knife in his hand. The walls were covered in blood. It was like something from a horror movie. I ran and hid in the bathroom until the police came.

They came and took him away to a mental institution, and we didn't see him again for a long time. I later learned that he thought my stepfather was having an affair with his wife. Through my studies of mental health today, I have learned that people who suffer this kind of mental illness tend to blame those closest to them for conspiring against them. In his mind, he thought that my stepfather was sleeping with his wife before she'd run off. I still suffer what I call Sudden Wakeup Fright, where, if I'm sleeping and I'm woken suddenly, I either want to—and have, on occasion—attack or flee before coming to my senses. To this day, I sleep in track pants, just in case. I believe the correct term for it is post-traumatic stress disorder (PTSD).

My uncle came back after a few years. Where before he could recognise his family and friends, he now seemed to be in his own world, swollen and pumped up with medication.

Disaster struck again. There were two sisters who lived up the street from us, Sharon and Ruby. They were good people, and we often hung out. One day, Sharon was pushing her baby carriage not too long after giving birth to her first daughter when she encountered my uncle walking toward them. He proceeded to snatch the baby from the carriage and began slamming the baby against the concrete ground. The police and an ambulance were called, and my uncle was taken away and committed to a mental institution, where he remained till his passing.

Sharon's baby didn't die from the incident, but I believe there were longterm health issues. She eventually moved from the neighbourhood, and I never saw her or her sister again. It was said that his reason for doing this was because, in his cognitive distorted thinking, he couldn't come to terms with losing his own child when his wife ran off and took his son, so he became enraged and bitter to the point at which seeing another child triggered his emotions, which quickly turned to rage.

From my uncle's experience, I learned that people should always protect their mental well-being because if they don't, it can have serious consequences for them and those close to them. Make no mistake—mental illness can happen to anyone, particularly if you are in a heightened and stressful state of mind for whatever reason, depending on your particular vulnerabilities and psychological make-up.

CHAPTER 4

Hooky

1977 WAS MY FIRST year in junior high school. I was thirteen going on fourteen. At that time, New York was plunged into darkness. It was called the Black Out of '77, and it lasted for three days. During that time, most if not all, grocery stores, liquor shops, appliance stores, and supermarkets were looted. Some friends and I looted the local liquor store not far from my house on Vanderbilt Avenue, and the next day, we sold so much liquor I couldn't find places to hide all the money. My momma accidentally found it in my closet, so I told her I'd found it, and she believed me as people were picking up all kinds of stuff off the streets. People were running around with TVs and stoves — I even saw a guy with a refrigerator on his shoulders, running down the street. I don't know how he managed it, but such was the time.

Before the lights came back on, thousands had been arrested in Brooklyn, not to mention the other boroughs, but as usual, Brooklyn was the hardest hit due to it being the biggest and baddest borough. However, almost everyone got something from the blackout. It was like a double serving of Christmas, only you got to choose your presents.

Around that same time, there was a serial killer running around New York. They called him Son of Sam. His method of killing was shooting random people with a .44 Magnum, a very powerful handgun. Everyone was watching their backs. He was eventually caught and turned out to be a mailman of Polish descent named David Berkowitz. He said his dog told him to do it. Some people still have doubts about his motive to this day.

During this period, at the end of the summer, I graduated from public school at a church called Washington Temple on Washington Avenue, where the civil rights activist Reverend Al Sharpton used to preach. From there, I started Rothschild Junior High School, one of the worst—if not *the* worst—junior high schools in Brooklyn. The students going there were from four predominantly Black neighbourhoods known as Fort Green.

Bedford Stuyvesant was also known as Bed-Stuy, Crown Heights, and Prospect Heights. Whites didn't go to our schools. I never went to a school with any white person; we were smartly divided by the powers that be. Like before, this segregation was done through the zoning of the school system, where children were only allowed to go to neighbourhood schools, and since there were no whites living in our hood, they didn't go to our schools and vice versa. These environmental and economic conditions — as well as the trauma — continued to shape and mould me.

Rothschild was located on Carlton and Dekalb Avenues in the heart of Fort Green, a volatile neighbourhood where people got shot for daring to walk through it or looking in someone's direction. There were police patrolling our school all day, which didn't help much, as robberies and muggings and fights continued daily. The cop patrolling the school was called West and he was about seven feet tall. I kid you not. Whenever there was a fight, he walked up, reached over the crowds, and plucked up the culprits.

I remember my first day in junior high. I was punched in the chest by one of the school bullies who wanted my lunch money. I told him I didn't have any, and he said, 'All I find I keep,' which was slang used on the streets when taking someone's property or valuables. His name was, of all things, Monkey Man, and I must say, I could see a resemblance. He told me to take off my sneakers, and he found my dollar folded in my sock. Needless to say, I missed lunch that day and went home hungry. There was no one to complain to; that was just the way it was.

A few weeks later, some friends and I were standing around outside on our lunch break when we heard the sound of glass crashing. Everyone headed in that direction to see what happened, and when I got close enough, I saw that it was our science teacher. It seemed that he was pushed out of the window by some students. I don't know why, and I don't know if he survived. He never came back, and I never saw him again. Also, around my second year,

I started to play hooky, which was skipping school and hanging out with my fellow hooky players. We even had hooky parties.

I liked the hooky parties as there were a lot of girls from our school who attended, and there was always the chance you could get lucky. I never did, but I suffered from an adultification of my childhood, that is, thinking and feeling like I was 'grown' because of the hard stuff and knocks life had dealt me for most of my childhood. Being fourteen years old, my mind had begun to settle on the birds and the bees. As the hooky group, we also spent a lot of days in Prospect Park, which is a very big park in the middle of Brooklyn. The Brooklyn Public Library was across the street, but that wasn't our focus. In the park, we'd fish in the lakes, smoke weed, drink beer, and have park rangers chase us around all day. By the way, my first introduction to weed smoking took place when I was five years old. I won't say who passed it to me. Not that I started smoking regularly from then on.

Very tragically, my best friend at the time, Jerome, drowned in one of those lakes we played in after a session of smoking weed and drinking alcohol. He decided he wanted to go for a swim, which the rest of us declined. I wasn't a swimmer, so it wasn't a hard decision for me. Jerome walked over to the lake by the skating rink and jumped in, and that was the last time we saw him alive. It took a few hours for them to fish him out. I never went back to the park for more than a year after that. It was another trauma to try to do something about on my own.

At the end of the year, it was time to get our report cards and take them home and get a lot of big hugs, but there was no such thing for me at Hooky High School. I had Long Term Absences (LTA) in every class report, *and* I had to get it signed by my moms. Getting my report card signed was always tricky business. I was versed in signing my mother's signature because I gave it a lot of practice. So, I signed it off, got away with it, and passed the test until it was Parent Teacher Association Day (PTA) in 1978, and there was no way around that.

When my mother came to my school, she was so surprised and totally unimpressed at how many school days I had missed. So much so that she decided to send me back to Jamaica as a punishment until I'd learned my lesson. On that day of action, I was hanging out in Fort Green Park with my friend, Trinity, when my brothers tracked me down and handed me over. It wasn't really a surprise that she took such drastic measures; Moms didn't play.

CHAPTER 5

The Return to Jamaica

I WAS PACKED UP and put on a plane to Jamaica two days after the PTA meeting. At that time, my grandmother's house, which was always full of cousins, was almost empty as everyone had already left for the USA to start their life's journeys. It was mainly me, my cousin Marky, his sister and my cousin, Diane, and Teddy. Things were hard financially at Grandma's, but we made the best of a bad situation. We had a lot of fruit to compensate for the lack of food. The Mocho Mountains, as that section of Clarendon, Jamaica, is called, was originally inhabited by German Jews and some Scottish and Irish, going back to Colonial days. I later found out that my great-grandfather and great-grandmother on my mother's side were Jews from Germany. Their name, Schroder, was changed and replaced with Shorter, who married Mary Drummond, and the rest is history.

I must say, it was around that time I met Anne, who lived in the community not far from our house. We spent a lot of time together when I was around as I also spent a lot of time in Montego Bay. I really looked forward to seeing her every chance I got. I can't explain it, but I really felt joy when we were together. We eventually branched out in different directions, but we remain in touch and great friends to this day.

Mocho has such rich soil that anything can grow there, and the weather is always sunny during the day and cool in the evenings. The soil is so rich in aluminium that a mining company called Alcoa bought up most of the land through the government and moved most of the community to different parts of the island, totally ruining the environment and community for the purpose of mining aluminium. Needless to say, the community has not yet recovered.

I spent one year in Jamaica, mainly because the US only gave non-citizens one year outside of the country as a policy. I went to Maypen High School for a while and also Lennon High in Mocho, the latter being one of my great-grandfather's Lennon-learning institutions.

After serving one year in exile, I was pardoned and allowed to go back to the USA with my mother making threats that any more bad reports and I'd be sent back. I was happy to head back to New York, but I knew I'd miss our little house on the hill and my cousins.

Upon my return to Brooklyn, I was picked up from the airport by my stepfather, a good but no-nonsense kind of man. He was a cop and fireman once upon a time in Jamaica. He read me the riot act on the way home. I agreed and signed it.

I was sent back to Rothschild Junior High, and it wasn't long before I was back to no good. The streets had me. It was my last year in junior high; the next year would be high school.

It was 1979 and my first day at high school, a step up from junior high and a whole new ball game. Me, Blocker, Coolie, Romie D, Howie, and Trinity decided to make our first appearance together. We signed a pact to watch each other's backs, just as we had since we became friends at Rothschild. I had a Trinidadian friend who lived on my street. He basically did his own thing, and what he did was repair and sell guns. If someone had a gun and it had issues, he'd fix it. I acquired a .25 Automatic: my first burner [GUN]. Taking turns, we picked each other up as we walked to our new school. I felt like a giant packing my first strap. I was seventeen years old. Trinity was already pressuring me to let him hold the gun at lunchtime, but I kind of held back where he was concerned as he was a kind of loose cannon, and I didn't want to give him a real one.

When we got to school, the Latinos (Puerto Ricans) had their spot, and the Yankees (Black Americans) had their spot. We found a spot where we could keep an eye on everyone as we didn't trust anyone. The doors opened, and we were allowed into the school. We didn't have to wait long, but we decided to let the crowd go ahead of us. Sarah J Hale was a massive school on Dean Street and 4th Avenue, and like the other schools, it was a zoned school, so everyone from the hood was basically on the same journey but with different visions. The school's name has since changed.

The day passed by relatively quietly without drama, but Trinity was still on me to hold the .25, so after school, I gave it to him to hold for the night. The next day, we heard that he went out at night to play dice, ended up accusing someone of cheating, and shot the place up. He was a real hot-head.

I decided to let Blocker hold it next. He was a serious guy who didn't smile much, and he would always have your back if needed. Things were good for a while until one day, we went outside to chill only to see that the Latinos had taken over our spot. We decided to check them.

I walked up, and before I could say anything, Blocker had the gun out, and people started running everywhere. Blocker fired off a few rounds in their direction, and we didn't see them again that day.

The next day, we were back at our spot outside chilling when we saw Larry headed in our direction. Larry was the local redneck cop who only picked on Blacks. He was school security. He came over, and we were smoking weed and drinking beer, as most people did at our school. He didn't see the weed, but he saw the beer, and he came over to tell me to pour it out.

I said, 'No,' because I'd paid for it, so I was going to finish it.

He threw a punch that I saw coming a mile away.

I ducked, Romie D grabbed him from behind and threw him on the ground, and we ran for our lives. Needless to say, we had to lay low for a while.

We stopped going to school for a good while, so we decided we needed more guns to start making real money. I went to my Trinidadian friend, who had two .38s and a .32 Auto. Trinity quickly took a .38, and I gave the other one to Coolie. Blocker liked the .25 as it was easy to conceal, and I took the .32 Auto. We had a plan to rob the neighbourhood numbers spot. The numbers spots were like gambling houses, except you bought three, four, or five numbers, and if, at the end of the day, those numbers were played, you won. Our first spot was owned by Scatter, an OG in the hood, but we didn't care who owned it.

The spot was on Underhill Avenue, and their security was bulletproof glass, so we either had to go early, when it was just opening, or later when they were closing. We decided on going early, so we got there at 8 a.m., the four of us. We waited until the man, who was one of the workers, opened the shutters and bent down to go in before we pounced and pushed him in. Trinity and I went in, mainly because I didn't want to leave him outside as he had a crooked look about him that might attract suspicion.

We locked the guy in the bathroom, but not before he saw our faces, and that was how Scatter knew it was us who had robbed the spot. We took a paper bagful of money from under the counter — it could have been a week's worth of takings — went back to my house and split the money four ways.

We robbed almost every numbers-spot in our neighbourhood. We had a few run-ins with Scatter as he owned most of the spots, but they were minor. I didn't see Trinity after that for a while, as by then we had officially stopped going to school and joined the statistics of high school dropouts.

It was just three of us left: me, Blocker, and Coolie (Romey D had gone to Florida with his moms). Howard started working with his uncle, doing mechanical work. Trinity was MIA, but we heard he had a new monicker (the new name of Stick Man, due to his robbing a lot of people). We opened a weed shop, and it was doing well. We would take other people's weed and sell it at our spot. By then, we were seasoned, hardened takers (crooks), and no one messed with us.

One day, a few months after we'd opened, Trinity came to see Blocker. I was surprised to see him. I heard he'd been up to all kinds of badness. He said he'd run out of bullets and needed some more. He wouldn't ask me because he knew I wouldn't give him any. Later that day, Coolie said he thought Blocker might have given him some.

A few days later, I was outside the spot chilling and checking out the shorties (girls) when a friend of ours, Ronald, came by to ask if we had heard what Trinity did. We hadn't. He went on to say that Trinity had gone with three so-called friends on a robbery in East New York. They got money and jewellery and went to a spot to chill for the night, but while everyone was asleep, Trinity woke up and shot each one of them in the head. Needless to say, we were all speechless. Such was the time. I think I was the only one he ever showed any kind of respect.

By that time, we had robbed most of the numbers, weed, and coke spots in Brooklyn, and people started calling us the Stickup Kids. It was around that time that I started rolling with my cousins in Flatbush. They pretty much had that side of town locked down. It was also around that time I became the father of a son.

PART TWO

CHANGING THE GAME

The Roll Back to the Tree

"

Sometimes people hold a core belief that is very strong. When they are presented with evidence that works against that belief, the new evidence cannot be accepted. It would create a feeling that is extremely uncomfortable, called cognitive dissonance. And because it is so important to protect the core belief, they will rationalise, ignore and even deny anything that doesn't fit in with the core belief.

~ Frantz Fanon, psychiatrist and political philosopher

"

CHAPTER 6

Life of Crime

I MET MY SON'S mother at the local skating rink on Empire Blvd. It was a place where people from different neighbourhoods met up mostly on the weekends to hang out, although few people actually skated, mostly the girls. I walked in on this particular Sunday night with Coolie and Ronald, and lo and behold, I saw the prettiest girl looking my way. When our eyes met, I knew I wanted her for the rest of my life; I can't explain it. I decided to keep walking to the back and stand by the snack shop — this was my spot whenever I went there. I felt someone standing behind me and looked around, and it was her. I said, 'Hi.'

She smiled, said, 'Hi,' and that was all she wrote.

We became an item. To me, she was the prettiest girl in Flatbush. Her name was Frederica, and she was Jamaican, and whenever we couldn't see each other, we were always on the phone.

I always kept spare change for the phone box as in those days we didn't have cell phones. It came to pass that she gave me my son Daniel, and eight years later, my daughter Kassandra. Kassandra hasn't spoken to me much since birth, maybe because I wasn't there for her at a young age when a child needs their dad the most, and although it hurts, I can't say I blame her, but that's another story.

I remember the day my son was born. I took Frederica to the hospital in downtown Brooklyn, Long Island University College Hospital. On the drive there, I became anxious about the future and what being a parent meant. I swiftly put those feelings away, focusing on what was about to take place: the delivery of my son.

Frederica's mother came to the hospital and decided she wanted to be in the room when the baby was born, but they only allowed one person in the delivery room. I put up some resistance for a while, but I soon gave in for peace's sake, and I waited outside until my son was born and they called me in.

After my son was born, Frederica and I moved to Harlem, and we lived at 117th and Lenox Avenue for a few months before moving back to Brooklyn. Harlem life was...let's just say that it wasn't our cup of tea. The neighbourhood was constantly buzzing with the cops and junkies, plus we felt more at home in a West Indian hood.

I loved my son very much. I particularly liked to put him on my shoulders and take him for walks in the park or to the store (shops). He was always an active kid, and more times than not, he would do the exact thing you told him not to. Frederica was the disciplinarian in our family. I could never physically discipline my son because I hated to see him cry or want for anything. I remember times when he'd misbehave, his mother would be getting ready to spank him, and I would pick him up, put him on my shoulder, and run off with him, laughing all the way.

After returning to Brooklyn at the age of 19 in 1985, my life took on a new meaning. I had responsibilities now. I had to step up my game. Frederica went back to her mother's and was living in Flatbush on Lenox Road, so now I had a place in Flatbush. Her mother didn't like me, perhaps for obvious reasons, so for a while, I didn't get to see my son and Frederica as much. She said I always looked sneaky and always walked with my head down as if I were hiding something. She wasn't far off.

I started hanging with my cousins and their crew, the Linden BLVD Crew, or the LBC as it was known then. My cousins and I grew up on that hill in Jamaica, so we basically had the same experiences in life and a shared vision. My cousin Bim and me started out by robbing every weed shop in Flatbush. There was one shop we robbed on a cold winter's day, complete with a snowstorm.

We walked in, ready for action, but as usual, we had to get them to open the bulletproof side door. So, I fired off a shot into the ceiling, and like magic, the door opened. We told the guy to lay down on the floor while we searched to find the weed and money. The mistake we made was not searching him before we left, which was a miscalculation on our part. We left the store and got about twenty feet before the guy ran out, shooting some kind of automatic handgun.

We turned and sent some shots in his direction before taking off down the road. We made it to my cousin's house on Cortelyou Road before all of the police sirens came due to the shooting. We decided to chill for the rest of the day. We'd dropped a very large gold ring in the melee, and Junior went back out in the snow to find it.

The next day, a friend of ours, called Banga, came to see us to say he had work (a robbery). It was a weed spot on Utica Avenue called Timbuktu, and it was run and controlled by dreads. No one had ever robbed the dreads or even attempted it. We hoped this might work in our favour as they wouldn't be on the lookout, and we could catch them sleeping, so to speak.

The next day, me, Banga, and my cousin Bim, walked in the shop. They sold records at the front of the shop, and there were two dreads behind the counter. Straight to the back was a two-way mirror where the person behind it could see you, but you couldn't see them. We knew that was where all the weed and money were, but the trick was getting the door opened without alarming whoever was behind the glass.

We walked in and started looking at some records while scoping out the place. We then made eye contact and walked casually to the counter with a couple of records. As we got to the counter, Banga calmly told the dread that we had guns on them so they shouldn't make any funny moves.

We decided to stand to the side and let them knock on the door, so we could rush in once the door had been opened. So, we stood on either side of the glass door, and the dread knocked on the door. It seemed as if they had a code knock because as we heard the first click of the lock, both dreads made a push at the door, and it opened wide. All we could see was about five or six dreads, all with guns aimed our way. When they started shooting, it sounded like the fourth of July. We couldn't run out because the exit door was in the direct line of fire, so to get out, we had to return fire while heading for the door and pray.

We made a rush for the exit, firing shots in their direction, and then I heard Banga yelp. After we'd made it through the door, we realised he'd been shot in the ass. We jumped into the car and headed home, where Banga's girl came to pick him up and take him to the hospital. They operated, but they couldn't take the bullet out as it was lodged in the soft tissue. The bullet is still there to this day.

It was a week later when I saw Blocker, and he asked me if I'd heard what happened to Trinity. I hadn't. He went on to say that Trinity was staying at someone else's girlfriend's crib (apartment), always the opportunist. She had her real man who was in jail and due to come home soon, and Trinity knew this because the girl had told him so.

It came to pass that the other man was released and went straight to his girl's house, as any red-blooded man would.

Blocker said that when the guy knocked, and Trinity answered the door, the guy asked him who he was and what he was doing in his girl's house. Trinity said a few choice words in Jamaican dialect, turned his back on the guy and was walking back in when the guy pulled a gun and shot him twice in the head. Charles, who was an OG in the hood that we all respected and had a very successful weed business called Serious Gold, chipped in on the donations to get him buried as his mother didn't want to know. I went to the funeral parlour to see him, and for the first time, I could actually say he looked peaceful. It was sad that the only peace to be found in the neighbourhoods was at the pearly gates (death's door).

CHAPTER 7

Death's Door

IN 1980, A GUY called Mel, who used to hang around with us at the time, supposedly shot someone in Park Slope, which is an upscale neighbourhood in Brooklyn. The police grabbed anyone and everyone. I was picked up and brought to the 78th Precinct, which is in that neighbourhood. I was taken to an upstairs back room in the precinct and had both legs chained and each arm handcuffed, so I was spreadeagled. The cop retrieved a picture, showed it to me, and asked if I had ever seen the guy before. I said I didn't, and the cop went into a cabinet and took out a very hard and thick rubber hose. He asked the question again: 'Have you seen this man before?'

I said I hadn't.

What followed was the worst beating I've had in my life. The first blow hit me in the face, and blood immediately covered my clothes and the floor. He asked the question many times, and each time I was hit with the hose. He then kicked me in the groin, after which I saw colours and stars. My face was a swollen, bloody mess, but still, I had nothing to say.

I was charged with resisting arrest and sent to Rykers Island. There's a law in New York that says the police don't have any lawful rights to assault you unless you resisted arrest, hence the bogus charges. When I got to the Island, everyone was amazed to see my face so swollen. I spent three weeks on remand before going to court. When I got to court, the judge looked at me sympathetically and asked if I had any complaints or issues against the cops. I said, 'No,' as I didn't need any more stress. The judge threw out the case because the cops had no justifiable reason to hold me, and they were being cagey about my actual charge.

It was now 1984. My son was three-years-old. My relationship with Fredrica was okay, but her mother still didn't like me much. Daniel was a good kid. He reminded me of me when I was still innocent. I liked to carry him around on my shoulders, and his favourite word was *Bibow*, mimicking the sound so many children in the hood grew up hearing and learning: the sound of gunshots. So, as a nickname, we used to call him Bibow.

Let me say a little about Spangy, one of our friends, albeit a disrespectful one. Spangy was killed around this time in the eighties. There's even a movie out about it called Crown Heights. His mother lived on Linden Blvd, so naturally, he was brought into our crew by Ricky, who was also from Spangy's old neighbourhood in Jamaica. He was a member of the Spanglers Gang in Jamaica, hence the name Spangy. He was a hothead and disrespectful to most people. He thought that because he'd come from a rough place in Jamaica, it gave him the right to disrespect whoever he felt like.

We also had a friend called Yankee. He was a Black American, but he was loyal, and he had your back in any given situation. We all liked him. He was one of us.

Yankee went on a burglary and stole a pearl-handled silver .32 Automatic, the prettiest gun we ever saw. We all liked to hold it and pose, and Yankee never said no. One day, Spangy asked Yankee to let him hold it to take a picture, and when Yankee gave it to him, Spangy walked off, said he was keeping it, and there was nothing Yankee could do about it. We were all vexed when we heard, but in the streets, Yankee had to defend his honour because it was an internal beef between them. That's just the way it was.

Three months went by, and most of us forgot about it as things moved so fast on the streets, but Yankee didn't. He told Spangy that he had a works (robbery), and he told Spangy an elaborate story about an apartment full of drugs, and he knew the people inside, so it should be a walk in the park. Spangy quickly agreed.

The next day, they went to an apartment building somewhere in Flatbush. Yankee took him to the top floor, and when Spangy turned his back, Yankee shot him in the head, killing him instantly. Yankee then took Spangy's red and white suede Puma sneakers and wore them as a badge of honour. He showed everyone the sneakers. We all knew what had happened, but to us, it was one man defending his honour. No more was said, but it turned out that a friend of Spangy's killed another friend of ours, Mario, because he thought Mario did it. The police actually locked up a Trinidadian guy who had nothing to do with it, and he served twenty years in prison before being exonerated and given a few million for a wrongful conviction after the real murderer later confessed to the crime.

I had just turned nineteen, and I was coming under a lot of pressure from my moms to stop what I was doing and think about my son, but to me, that's why I was out there in the first place, to provide for my son. Anyway, I decided to enrol in a trade school in downtown Brooklyn on Atlantic Avenue, Burke Trade School. I wanted to do plumbing, so I went through the preliminaries and enrolled. It was me, Ricky, and a friend of mine who went on to become a famous reggae artist in New York (Bobo General). I actually made it a whole week there before I was sent to Ryker's Island for six months for robbing someone's gold chain. Previously, I had been sent to Ryker's Island on other cases, though I was not there for long.

I was hanging with my friend, Little Jack, when a guy walked past us, wearing a rope chain. Jack said, 'Let's get that,' so I ran up to the guy and grabbed the chain, only to see a police car coming towards us, lights flashing. They had seen the whole thing.

Jack walked off. They had only seen me. I was arrested and sent to Ryker's Island, the infamous C74, a total madhouse where the guards turned a blind eye to everything for a quiet life. The inmates ran the place. I wasn't worried as I had many friends there, and I could handle myself, which I did.

I was sent to C76 from C74 after being convicted. C74 houses are mostly remands. C76 is a dormitory holding about six hundred inmates, who were separated into Bronx, Brooklyn, Queens, and Manhattan. So, if you were from Brooklyn, that's the section you would go to. I spent three weeks there before being sent to Potter's Field, a little island outside of the Bronx. You need a barge to get there. My job was to bury dead people for the state. The name has since changed to Hart Island. Potter's Field was a place where John Does or the homeless were buried. The state used inmates to do the work and paid a little better than the regular jail pay at Rykers, and you were outside most days, so it was okay. I did my time digging graves, collected my chump change, and when I was released, I headed back to the hood. Needless to say, my position at Burke Trade School had expired.

When I got home from jail, my cousin, Tony (Bam), came to see me, telling me about this new high called free-basing that we should start selling. We got an ounce and started selling and making good money for a while. I always saved the dust and scraps from the leftovers after packaging the crack cocaine. I collected it and put it in a spliff. I did this for a period before getting hooked, and I started getting high on my own supply. I was twenty years old when I got hooked on crack.

I tried to maintain some discipline, but it wasn't long before I realised I was out of control. I was hooked. My cousin, Bim, also smoked bazookas — that's what we called it in a spliff. I graduated to the pipe, which is the worst as it is more extreme and highly addictive. I smoked my money from work, and now I was back on the streets, robbing to feed my habit. Sometimes, I didn't shower for days, and that only happened when I went to my mom's house. I remember smoking with a friend, and I gave him the money to buy some more, and he never came back, so I went looking for him. I found him at a girl's house. I asked him what happened, and he tried to make up a story, so I punched him in the face a couple of times, and that's when he pulled out a knife and stabbed me in the chest.

I didn't even realise I was stabbed until someone said that I'd better go to the hospital. That's when I looked down, saw the blood, and realised I was bleeding. I walked off and flagged a taxi to the hospital.

I collapsed outside of the hospital, and my friend Coolie from school days, who had actually seen everything and came with me to the hospital, had to go inside to get a wheelchair to push me in as the doctors weren't allowed to come outside to bring me in. I think it had something to do with insurance. This was at the Brooklyn Jewish Hospital on Prospect Place. The name has since changed to Interfaith.

My heart stopped beating twice, and they used electric shock treatment to revive me. I was in the hospital for two months with a punctured lung. I remain ever grateful to the doctors. One of them shook my hand and told me how lucky I was, as it was touch and go that I'd survive.

I went to stay at my mother's house as my girl's mother didn't want me anywhere near her house. I saw my son occasionally during those days and got to hang with him at the park sometimes.

By then, my mother told me that I had been born in England and that maybe I needed to leave New York for a while as I had the police looking for me and I had some of the underworld trying to catch up with me. At that time, England never crossed my mind as I had mostly grown up in Jamaica and the USA.

I took her advice and went to the British Embassy in Washington as they had moved from the city to Washington. I applied and got a passport. My mother bought a ticket, but at the last minute, I didn't want to leave my son, so I decided to take him and his mother with me because she wouldn't let me take my son if she hadn't come, which was okay with me. We got married, and then we all left together.

We got on the plane in 1985 and landed in London, Heathrow, where my cousins and my uncle came to pick us up. They lived in the northwest section of London. My uncle got me a job working for British Rail as a trackman engineer on Liverpool Street. I worked and made good money. In those days, we got paid in cash in a little brown envelope.

Things were okay until my wife wanted to go live in Bristol, where her brother lived. I didn't want to leave London, and the decision caused arguments. Eventually, she left for Bristol with my son. I remained in London for a few months after she left, and I started to feel isolated and alone. I bought a ticket and headed back to New York, which I missed, as it felt more like home.

I arrived in Brooklyn and headed immediately back to familiar territories. By that time, 1987, the neighbourhood was becoming a ghost town as more and more people were getting hooked on crack cocaine. I started smoking again, only this time around, I was totally bombed out. The next few years went by in a blur. While all I wanted was to quit the habit, it was easier said than done. I often felt suicidal after each crack session as my life felt and got more and more out of control. Sometimes, I'd even go so far as to smash the pipe and throw out all of the paraphernalia, only to buy a new set the next day. My life was a mess.

I was sent back to Ryker's Island for breaching probation after getting into trouble with the law again to feed my habit. I was given two years. It was at that time I decided never to smoke crack again, and to do that, I had to leave the hood and the people I had once hung out with, which was hard. That decision, I believe, changed my life and unsealed my fate of becoming another tragic statistic.

CHAPTER 8

Stirrings of Change

AFTER RETURNING TO BROOKLYN from the UK in 1999, I went to stay with my moms, who had two houses in Flatbush. She was happy when I came home because she needed the help maintaining and managing the properties, and of course, she was happy to see me. It always warms my heart to see my mom's smile. I didn't mind helping as it gave me a sense of contributing to all she does for me.

After a few months, I decided I needed a little more financial stability, so I applied for a security job. I got the job a few weeks later and started working as a security guard in downtown Brooklyn at the Williamsburg Bank, which later became HSBC. It is a thirty-three-storey building and has a clock on each side at the top, so anywhere you are in Brooklyn, you can see the clock. I started out patrolling the building, doing what's known as the Graveyard Shift: twelve midnight to seven in the morning. I did this for a while before becoming a supervisor for the night shift, in charge of seven security officers. It was a good job, and I enjoyed it, but the money wasn't worth all the sleepless nights and the abuse from the customers and staff.

I did that for three years until a friend of mine suggested that I could make more money driving an ambulance, transporting patients to and from dialysis and other medical appointments. I applied and got the job. I really liked the job as it gave me a sense of purpose and made me feel like I was actually helping people and giving back. I did the night shift, which seemed to be a pattern of mine. Most drivers were afraid to do the night shift due to their being robbed and assaulted on a regular basis. The streets of Brooklyn, particularly at night, can be a tricky place to navigate where crime was concerned. I didn't mind because I knew and understood the streets.

I liked my job so much that sometimes, I'd go above and beyond my duties for the patients. There was a Jewish lady, Miss Lowenthal, who I used to take to the dialysis centre on McDonald Avenue, and she lived on the 12th floor. Sometimes, when the elevator was broken, I walked up the stairs to bring her down in a wheelchair, one step at a time; she smiled all the way down. She was one of my favourite service users as she never complained. Sometimes, I'd do a double shift if someone didn't come in that day, and one of these days, I drove down my old block, saw Louie, and heard that everyone from the old hood was gone, one way or another: prison and/or death.

In 2001, I met my second wife, Betty, who worked in a liquor store on Bedford Avenue. She was Trinidadian mixed with Spanish Venezuelan. She was very pretty, and she had a good heart, which I particularly liked. She was also a hard worker, but she had a fiery temper, which caused us a lot of unnecessary arguments. After spending most of our time together in a room on 98th Street in Flatbush, we decided to get married. Later, we got an apartment together on Church Avenue, a busy main street that ran through Flatbush in Brooklyn.

In 2002, I really started to see life in a more mature and thoughtful way. I was tired of my previous behaviours, habits, and routines, and I needed change in my life, so I gradually started to do things in a different way. For example, before, I would wake up in the morning and light up a spliff, but I stopped doing that as it made me lethargic and slow-minded, definitely a bad way to start your day. I decided not to smoke until after work, or after all of my daily chores were done for the day. I also decided to not hang out with friends as much as before and to use the time to visit the gym and run in Prospect Park. I was tired of jail, police, probation, parole, hard drugs, and all the things that were responsible for my failing myself, my life, and my children.

As I already mentioned, I got a job as a security guard in downtown Brooklyn. I did the graveyard shift, and by the time I got home around ten in the morning, I'd be dead tired. I would sleep most of the day, eat, shower, and head out to work again.

Although it was tough in the beginning, I grew into the job and was happy when I became a supervisor.

I applied and got another job working at UPS in Maspeth, Queens, during the day, so I left security, jumped on the train to Queens, and rested in brief intervals on the train between stops to work. It wasn't easy. I actually fell asleep one day and woke up in the Bronx, a long way off track, so to speak. But in a funny kind of way, I enjoyed the change because everything was new and different. I was beginning to see and learn that there was a different life out there that didn't include the police or any of the aforementioned people and organisations involved in my chastisement.

I know there are a lot of youths out there feeling stuck in a situation that seems to have no escape, especially where peer pressure is concerned, but let me say that you have to take control of your actions, thoughts, and attitude. Don't allow yourselves to be directed and guided or defined by others who may or may not have your best interests at heart. You have to be strong and focus on what you want and what's good for you as we are all on our own individual journeys in life with our individual lessons to learn. That reminds me of Von and his little brother Chris.

Around the corner from my house on Tilden Avenue lived a guy called Von, and it came to pass that Von used to hustle out in South Carolina, and he was killed for stepping on the next man's territory, meaning he started doing business (selling drugs) in a next man's patch without permission, and that's definitely seen as a disrespect. Von's little brother Chris used to walk by my house with his friends every day, and because I was someone from the streets—though somewhat retired—I could see that although Chris was rolling with the pack, he didn't feel the streets as much as his friends did.

I called him over as he passed by one day and asked him why he was walking with those guys. He told me that they went to school together. I said that wasn't a good excuse, especially if he could end up in jail or something worse. I asked him about school, and to my surprise, he was happy to tell me that he wanted to go to college, and we spoke a while about that before he left.

I saw him every day, and I always called him and deliberately had a long conversation with him about school, family, and his coping with his brother's death among other things. More times than not, his friends would leave him, which was my intention. We spoke about his desire to go to university to further his studies after college and his fear of failing. I spoke to him about not letting fear get in the way of progress as he had nothing to fear but fear itself.

We spoke regularly for many months until one day, he didn't come around, and I didn't see him again until about a year later. I was standing in front of my house on Church Avenue, and he walked up to me with a big smile and gave me a high five. I asked him where he'd been as I hadn't seen him. He said that he was in college in New Jersey, and he wanted to come by to say thank you to me, as he was grateful for our talks, and he didn't think he could have done it without our little talks. We talked for a while before he left.

I never saw him again, but I had a good feeling of accomplishment in the sense that I was influential in steering a yute (Jamaican patois for young person) in the right direction. Oftentimes, all we need is someone to listen, understand, and lend a hand.

I basically and deliberately used myself, sharing my experiences as examples of how not to get caught up in the game of life. I had to put myself down through my experiences to bring him up.

However, although things were looking up, things were about to change for me. I was at work on that fateful night, around 3 a.m., when a team of officers from Immigration Custom Excise (ICE) came to see me at work to arrest me for violating a visa waiver, meaning I'd overstayed my welcome. I was surprised, to say the least.

I was imprisoned in Monmouth County Jail, New Jersey, for three months, and directly after that, I was put on a plane to the UK. I believe the correct term is deportation.

It broke my wife's heart, and mine too, but we had to tough it out and move on with life. I learned from my experiences in life that shit happens, and my solution is to keep moving forward, physically, mentally, and spiritually. One of my favourite sayings is that no one ever moves forward standing still, and I stand by that.

After a few failed attempts at trying to get my wife to come to England, we decided to call it quits. The stress and the hurt were too much for us, so we decided to let it go; although we remained friends via Facebook for a while until she moved on, and I was happy for her.

The county jail provided some courses through the education department, and one such course was on post-traumatic stress disorder (PTSD). I wanted to know more about that as I'd heard about it before through friends, and it sounded like something I could relate to. I signed up only to learn that I had been suffering from this condition all of my life as a result of the many traumas I'd experienced early in life.

Months after arriving in the UK, I was arrested for something I had done when I was last in England and sent to Wandsworth Prison. Once, again, I held myself down and did my time, passing most of my time, as I usually did, self-improving. I read many an influential book while in jail, like the autobiography of Marcus Garvey, a must-read for anyone seeking a focus, perspective, or knowledge of self, culture, and inspiration. Other books were Malcolm X's life story, Harriet Tubman's, Nelson Mandela's, Oprah Winfrey's, Makaveli and many others, both fiction and non-fiction. I encourage anyone and everyone to read books as they open the mind to many wonders and information from different perspectives.

One of my favourite books is a book called *We Are All Doing Time, A Guide For Getting Free*, by Bo Lozoff and his wife Sita. It's a book about life, meditation, and coping strategies. It's also spiritual without being religious, an excellent book for those seeking an alternative to conventional ways of thinking and approaching life's daily ups and downs. I even read a great book a long time ago, written by a guy called De Lawrence, who taught how to use your mind to achieve your will, a very strong and powerful book. The book was banned worldwide and taken out of circulation; my uncle Linval was the only one I knew who had a copy.

Being in jail helped me come off crack back in the USA and the UK, and it helped me work on self-improvement. It also helped me with my anger problem. Well, jail provided the opportunity, should I decide to take it, to better myself. Sometimes, good can come out of a bad thing.

In the early years of my experiences with incarceration, I was very angry and always got into trouble one way or another. Because of that, more times than not, I was transferred to a new facility whenever I was too boisterous. I was always prepared for whatever came my way, and most of the time, it was a beat down (beaten up) from screws and/or CO's.

What started the change in my attitude and understanding of my anger problem was when I was sent to Redding Prison (closed now). I arrived and was immediately placed in the segregation unit (Seg or Block). I was on something called the six-month laydown, meaning I would do twenty-eight days in six allocated prisons in the segregation unit. I should say that most Seg units only had a mattress and a cardboard table and chair. I once knew a guy who had lost all of his hair after doing a six-month laydown. When he came back, he never misbehaved again. A laydown, so to speak, can do that to you. It's psychologically stressful as there's no contact with anyone. It's also physically taxing as the food ration is sparse, so you tend to lose a lot of weight by being so malnourished. The Bible was the only book you were allowed, along with minimal human contact.

Anyway, when I arrived at Redding, I was taken to the segregation unit and given a toothbrush and a bucket. To me, everything seemed normal as this was the usual protocol, but I didn't get any of the usual bullying from the screws in reception (CO's), which, to me, was a little odd.

I was in my cell for a couple of hours when the governor himself came to see me and introduced himself. He actually shook my hand and introduced himself, which is something I had never experienced from anyone behind the wall. He was about to close the door when he said that they got the newspaper there daily, so if I was interested, I could ask one of his staff to fetch me one.

"Okay," I said. I stood there for a few seconds. After he left, I thought it was cool, but there had to be something more to the niceties.

The next day, he came back to ask how I was doing. He said that there weren't a lot of people in the segregation unit at the moment, so instead of having a half-hour exercise in the yard, I could have an hour.

I said thanks again and stood in my cell, trying to figure out where the anger I was used to getting from the system was.

The following day, he again came to see me to ask how I was doing.

"Okay," I said.

He said there was an old TV somewhere that he could make available if I wanted to watch it.

I said, "Sure," as it had been a long time since I had watched television. I had an hour of exercise, and now I was getting to watch TV. This, to me, was too good to be true.

He came back a few days later to ask if everything was okay. As usual, I said, "Yes," only this time, I couldn't meet his eyes. I started to feel as if maybe I was a bad guy. I can't fully explain it, but that's how it felt. He then went on to say that he hadn't had any bad reports about me in the two weeks since I'd been there, so he was willing to give me the benefit of the doubt and put me in A Wing, which was a normal location. It meant I could have visits, go to the gym and library, and access all the other things the prison provided.

I was so grateful. I never misbehaved or got placed on report again in that facility, as I felt like I would have been letting the governor down after all he had done for me. I say this because sometimes in life, we don't always have to fight fire with fire. Sometimes, we can fight fire with water. This message is for all of us, I guess.

Furthermore, I got a better grip on my anger when I did that anger management course during my time in the UK jail. I was practically forced by the staff to do an anger management course, which I didn't think I needed as I didn't think I had a problem with my anger, but for one reason or another, I was regularly placed on report for aggressive behaviour or bullying. I was introduced to the course by the prison probation officer, who thought I needed intervention. The course turned out to be a real eye-opener in that it's not so much about how you see things but how others perceive, receive, and react to your approach, or interactions that seem innocent in your eyes, so to speak. For example, I was being reported by other inmates for bullying, and I couldn't understand why. On the course, in one of the sessions, there was a video camera installed, and I was asked to approach someone in the group in my normal fashion and ask for a roll up. Smoking was allowed in prison then. I must say, at the time, I weighed two hundred pounds (14 ½ stones) and was five foot six inches of solid muscle as I attended the gym regularly, so I was kind of an imposing figure. Anyway, I approached the guy in the role play with me and asked for a roll-up in my usual customary manner and sat back down.

The video was played back, and I saw my approach and body language, and to tell the truth, *I* would have given me whatever I asked for! I was totally surprised and amazed at how my body language and approach made me seem angry, aggressive, and intimidating, although it wasn't by conscious intention. It was more unconscious, something I'd picked up way back when for survival on the streets of Brooklyn, especially as we were being bullied for being West Indians.

From that course, I learned that sometimes, you couldn't see what others could, and it is crucial for you to be aware and conscious of your mental frame in your everyday dealings with others as your mindset can have a negative impact on—and outcome for—an otherwise positive intention. That lesson sticks with me today, and I continue to learn from it.

I also found a way to get quiet time in prison when I needed to get away from the inmates and screws alike. I have times when I feel a desperate need to get away from all of the hustle and bustle. I think I have always been an introvert deep down. I like and appreciate the time I have away from everyone, which is why on many occasions whilst locked up, I routinely made requests to be taken to solitary, or segregation, depending on the country I was in. Anyway, the system does not grant requests for solitary unless there is an infraction, as solitary confinement is used as punishment. For some such as myself, the rules can be altered somewhat, for peace's sake, so to speak, meaning that the screws were happy to put me out the way like that. It was during one of these requests for solitary confinement that I read that influential book I mentioned, *We Are All Doing Time*. It was there I learned and practised meditation.

I had to hide these more positive influences and changes, as well as my being a thinking and caring person by nature coming up, as being your true self was out of the question in *child* **Hoods**. Since then, I have become the kind of person who pays a lesson forward. I was a Listener in prison, which is an organisation developed by prisons where inmates can have one of their peers listen to them when they are stressed out for whatever reasons. By nature, I am also an empathic man, which is why, when I was offered the listener's job in prison, I jumped at it because I could understand and relate to the ups and downs of life. God knows I've experienced my share, spread on thick. These days, more times than not, I care about the universal pain and struggles of life. I try to do my share of lending a healing hand wherever and whenever I can.

It always amazes me how the very things we sideline in life turn out to be the very things that are important to our growth and longevity. In my case, it was hiding my true self and trying to show my tough or hard side gained from life experience. As the saying goes, *'the stone that the builders reject has become chief cornerstone'* (Psalm 118:15-27)

My journey and my experiences throughout my life have served to give me a clear vision moving into the future. I am no longer always angry or arrogant and dissociated from people and the community at large. I now use empathy in my daily life as a means to put myself in someone else's shoes. I also use the consequences, gains, and losses way of problem-solving in which you measure your gains against your losses for any action that negatively affected you in the past, to learn future lessons.

I am also aware that we reap what we sow in this life; this is what we call the universal law. We answer to the universe for whatever actions and folly and/or harm we perpetrate. Life is about doing your best to live well with the universe and cause as little harm as possible as rest assured, it will come back to you. Which reminds me of a quote, 'Karma has no menu. You get served what you deserve,' ~Unknown.

I have done many courses over the years, for which I am grateful to have been given the opportunity. I have learned to take from each course and apply it to different situations in my life, and I hope that others may learn from my shared experience.

Thinking skills, anger management, victim awareness, and life skills are all helpful in daily life, and if a person has a good, strong network of family and friends, it's priceless. Being able to talk to someone about how you feel or what you are going through can actually have a positive effect on how you approach situations. They say that a problem shared is a problem halved. I have found this to be very true.

CHAPTER 9

To the Foundation

ANOTHER IMPORTANT LIFE EXPERIENCE for me in prison that gave me pride in my Black history and the contributions we have made on the world stage was the first ever Black history month celebration at Wandsworth Prison and the part I played in it. It was organised and put together by myself and a few people from the education department. I wanted to encourage and empower the Black community behind the walls. The Muslims have Ramadan, the Jews have Hanukkah, so I wanted to use Black history month to encourage Africans and West Indians that we, too, have occasions when we celebrate our culture, history, spirituality, and our ancestors who fought the good fight so we could survive to be here today.

We received a lot of pressure from the governor and staff, whose intentions were to discourage the celebrations, but we kept up the pressure, and in the end, we won the right to host the event. I was working in the kitchen at the time along with Miss Walker, a female Black member of the prison kitchen staff. She was instrumental in creating and accessing materials I couldn't, like photocopying, lobbying the governor, organising the gospel choir, and helping to print the magazine. I don't think I could have done it without her assistance; she was our rock.

Me and some friends who worked in the kitchen, prepared different Caribbean dishes, and we celebrated Black history month with gospel choirs from Pentecostal churches who sang songs to lift the soul and spirit. We even had a member of the Jamaica High Commission of UK come to the prison to do a question and answer session with the inmates, who had a lot of questions concerning their potential deportation to Jamaica.

Overall, the celebrations went well. The governor made a statement after the event that no more Black history month celebrations would be held at Wandsworth due to white and Asian inmates complaining that the Blacks were receiving preferential treatment, even though they themselves celebrated Ramadan and Christmas, with no complaints from the Black community and inmates there. I say all of this to say that we—Black folks—as a people need to stand up and fight for our rights as no one will fight for us. I personally have seen and experienced the attacks my Black family faces every day and are still very much facing today.

This brings to mind my first year in junior high school, which was a learning experience in many ways, some good and some bad. I was in the seventh grade in one of my favourite classes: social studies. I really liked to listen to the stories of old and history and imagine what it was like a thousand years ago. I should say that in those days, the Rasta Movement was on the rise in the Jamaican community and elsewhere. With it came Black Consciousness and the teachings of Marcus Garvey, including the truth and rights messages in music and the Jamaican- and British-American culture overall, which I was very much into.

During this political and historical time, one day, I walked into my social studies class and took my usual seat. The teacher started to talk about a guy called Amerigo Vespucci, who supposedly discovered America, and my question to the teacher was: 'How can he discover a country that was already discovered? The Indians were already there.' I didn't wait for an answer but decided to ask a question I had a burning desire to ask. I stood up and asked, "Why is it that you never teach anything about Black civilisation?" The whole class fell quiet as this was a subject often spoken about outside of school in haze-filled rooms, where we Black folks knew why.

The teacher stopped talking and stood still, looking at me. This prompted me to ask the question again, which I did.

The teacher walked up to me and told me that I was being disruptive and that I should leave class and report to the dean's office. I left the class, but I did not go to the dean, who was one notch under the principal; he could have me suspended. Anyway, I left school that day and laid low.

The next day, I didn't report to social studies class. I felt like the class wasn't relevant because I was being taught everyone else's history except for mine. I felt belittled and irrelevant, as if the African race hadn't contributed to mankind when it had in all kinds of ways. Even then, I realised that miseducation and history were recipes for underdeveloped minds, not for those interested in a real education, learning, and discussion, let alone reparation.

Add (unhealed) trauma into the mix, like the ones I had experienced in common with Black folks; it's no wonder that Black people go through life in survivor mode, struggling psychologically and economically from day to day. Due to what I know now about Adverse Childhood Experiences, Black folks continue to experience inequality and discrimination, and in later life, as adults, they are prone to experience disproportionately higher incidences of physical health issues and psychological ill health compared to white counterparts in the population. This disproportion also showed up again in the 2020 pandemic that was COVID-19, when research in England quickly showed that Covid-19 mortality rate for people of Black African or Black Caribbean ethnicity, was three times higher in comparison with white males and females. No surprise to us black folks. The same way it's no surprise to us that our story is nowhere to be found anywhere in the Western world's curriculum of History. Not our true story anyways. Just western society ways of seeing and misperceiving.

Yes, the odds have been stacked against us far outside of our making, but in the areas of collective progression and optimal human development, it is as this quote reminds us,

"

Survival mode is supposed to be a phase that helps save your life. It is not meant to be how you live. Survivor-mode is very taxing on the nervous system and adversely affects wellbeing—mentally, emotionally, spiritual, and physically.

~ Michele Rosenthal

"

As a people we have been in survivor mode for four hundred-plus years!

On an encouraging note, this also brings to mind another quote that can help us with building resilience, especially during these times

"

The same boiling water that softens the potato hardens the egg. It's what you're made of. Not the circumstances.

~ Unknown

"

CHAPTER 10

No Man Is an Island

AFTER MY RELEASE FROM jail, I was sent to a parole or bail hostel in Camden. There were around twenty-five guys there with the shared experience of prison. We were allowed to leave at 9 a.m. and return by 9 p.m. unless we had jobs and we could prove it. We also had to sign in and out. I never felt comfortable or free in the hostel due to the ins and outs of the police's revoking parole or bail for minor things such as breaking the 9 p.m. curfew by a matter of minutes. To me, it was a kind of mini-prison. Fortunately for me, I have always been an early riser and somewhat disciplined. I left the hostel every day at 9 a.m. and went around to building sites, looking for work.

Whilst looking for work, I was also eager to find somewhere to live and build a foundation. I eventually got a job through the help of St Mungo's Organisation, working with a construction company called Quinn, as a labourer. They were the best guys I ever worked with. Although I had to listen extra carefully when they spoke as they had deep, Northern Irish accents; more times than not, I just tried to get the gist of what was said and take it from there. Over a few weeks, I'd saved enough to rent somewhere affordable, a flat off of Goldhawk Road on Wendell Street in Shepherd Bush. It was a nice place, and it was mine.

Wendell Street was a quiet street; it even boasted a cooking school by a lady who was actually on TV as a chef. I really liked Shepherd Bush Westfield Mall, Holland Park, the clubs, and Pecking's Record Shop. I should say here that George 'Peckings' brought the first ever Soundclash to England and helped Coxsone Dodd to establish Studio One. Peckings came to the UK in 1960 and built a distribution network for Studio One and others leading to opening his shop in 1973. I spent a lot of free time hanging with Duke and talking about back in the day. I spent two years in the Bush before I had to move due to a high rent increase. I had a friend who lived in North London, and the rent wasn't bad on that side of town, so I decided to make the move.

I got a studio flat from a Chinese family living on my friend's street. They were very nice people. I still had my job, so the rent wasn't a problem. The only issue was taking the train to and from work every day as the Central Line was hot and packed, especially during rush hour. Still, I'd grown up in New York, which was probably one of the most crowded cities on earth, so I was able to navigate. I felt I had formed my roots and was building on them.

I guess you could say I beat the statistics. Oftentimes, I was told, growing up in my type of *child HOOD*, that I wouldn't make it to twenty-one as an African-American male. The system—and even the teachers at my school—preached and taught that our life expectancy was twenty-one, and a lot of us actually believed the rhetoric and ended up succumbing to an early death because we believed their miseducated, racist statements. Here I was at fifty, changing up my life and giving myself a better chance at a good life going and growing forward.

I was a little more fortunate than some guys at the hostel because I had a support network, which is very important for anyone facing resettlement or struggles in life. I have a big family and a few loyal friends who I can call upon to talk to or seek advice. It's a good thing to have a foundation to stand on. The reggae singer Dennis Brown said it perfectly in his song—'No Man is an Island', so developing and having a strong support network is important. It reminds me of a friend who had and lost the support of his family and friends.

His name was Tapon, and I met him in jail. He was a Hindu Indian and a very good soccer player. He was also a kind and humble guy. We often linked up in the yard and walked and talked about life, economics, politics, and religion. He was one of the few people able to discuss these topics rationally without getting too emotional, so I looked forward to our talks. He told me how important the family unit was in his country. He said that his family no longer spoke to him because he'd brought shame upon them by being in jail, so he got no visits, letters, or phone calls.

He had an expensive watch, and I used to jokingly ask him to sell it to me. He told me it was a gift from his father, who had died, and it was all he had to remember him by.

Tapon was a real cool guy. One day, we were in the yard, and he came over to me and said, 'D...I want to give you this watch as a token of our friendship.' At first, I thought he was joking, but then I quickly realised he wasn't joking. He kept trying to give me the watch, and I kept saying no. The bell rang to return to our cell blocks, and we touched fists before he left for the last time.

The next morning, there was a delayed unlock due to an emergency somewhere in the jail. I heard through the prison vines that there was a suicide somewhere in the jail, which was a kind of regular happening, so I dismissed it, mostly to protect my own sanity. I found out from an officer that they had found my friend Tapon hanging in his cell with some cloth stuck in his mouth. I couldn't believe it. I had just talked to him the day before. I later found out that his offering me his watch was a classic signal that a person might be contemplating suicide. They usually give their possessions away. This goes back to what I was saying about how important it was to have some kind of support network, be it family, friends, or just someone you can trust and talk to.

I feel like I needed to share his story as proof that no man can stand alone. We all need each other in many ways, even if it's just to talk. I appreciate my support networks today, and I do not take them for granted.

• CHAPTER 11 •

No More Drama

SINCE ARRIVING BACK IN England, doing my time, and resettling, I have remained relatively low-key, going to work and heading straight home after. I enjoy the quiet evenings at home alone without any drama, just like Mary J Blige sang about.

Other positive influences in my life were my mother and stepfather. My mother, especially, was a strong Black woman who, as well as raising six children, was a shrewd businesswoman. The only problem was that I did not listen to her advice and always had to learn the hard way. My mother was also a no-nonsense woman who didn't waste time. She was always doing something. One day, she said to me that whenever you have something to do, just do it, and don't leave things for later. From what I can remember, my mother was always a positive, confident woman and an almost larger-than-life character, and I must say, very religious. She did not suffer fools lightly.

My mother was into property, buying, selling, and renting houses. I remember people from the community coming to our house to see her for advice about buying a house, and she would sit them down and educate them about the property business. I, myself, learned a lot just by being around her. I sometimes collected rent from tenants and did some building maintenance. I truly believe that had I listened to my mother's advice throughout my life, I could have gone to the moon and back. She was not perfect, and she could speak to you quite harshly if you messed up, but she fulfilled her role of mother, as any Black mother can in this uneven and unequal land. She was a hardcore survivor, and I respect her for that. It had a positive bearing on me.

My stepfather, Mr Baugh as we called him, was a real father in every sense of the word. I remember my first day of school in the USA. I was terrified, to say the least, especially with the language barriers and the fact that my dress code was way off due to the reject sneakers I wore. They had cost a dollar and ninety-nine cents at our local John's Bargain Store on Flatbush Avenue, and anyone caught wearing a pair would be laughed at. Financially, things were tight for my family at the time. Upon entering school, my stepfather told me not to worry or be afraid as all of this — all of the hard knocks — would pass in time. He spoke that to me, which was reassuring. Within their relationship, the only problem they had was with his drinking and mismanagement of money. Because of that, my mother took over the management of finance in the household.

There was also the time I left my first wife in England and went back to USA due to my wife's moving to Bristol. I was heartbroken when I arrived, and my stepfather sat me down and explained that when I decided to get married, I didn't get a guarantee that things would work out. He was always there for me throughout my life, just like a real father.

I never saw my biological father until I went to England, and that was only briefly, in Harlesden, London. I waited a whole lifetime to meet him, and when I did, I ended up feeling worse afterwards as, in my mind, I had built it into a great reunion where he would have hugged me and told me how sorry he was for not getting in touch and not being in my life. Instead, he didn't say much, nor did he try to explain away my years of wondering and hoping. I needed to know who I was biologically and extended-family-wise, but that was not forthcoming. I left him that day feeling nothing. I came to realise that I already had a great father and didn't need another that late in life. I always give thanks for my life, but I came to realise that my father was just a sperm donor.

Over the years, the relationship between my son and me has had its ups and downs. We have times when we disagree on some topics and subjects, such as religion or politics. We even have debates about who's the best rapper. To him, I am old school, and he is of the new persuasion. We don't always see eye-to-eye, but that's okay, as every man or woman has their own perspectives and views, and they are entitled to them in life with no love lost. I have always tried to be a good father to him, especially since turning my life around. I had missed years of his childhood due to being in "second childhood" myself; the kind Nas the rapper sings about in his album

My son's mother now resides in Jamaica, and from time to time, we have catch-ups about what the children are up to. On a more disappointing note, I haven't seen or spoken to my daughter in many years, and to tell you the truth, we never really had a relationship. We had missed opportunities to bond when the bonding was important. It is one of the casualties of being caught up in prison life. I have made a few attempts to make a good connection over the years to no avail. I wish it could have been different, but such is the hand that was dealt. The last time I heard, she was pursuing her career and doing a good job, and for that, I thank the universe!

My moms died September 2016. On that fateful day, when I received the call that my mother had died, I couldn't find the words to fully express my feelings. I knew she was in her eighties, so I should have been somewhat prepared for the inevitable, but I wasn't. Instead, I was numb and in shock. I always kind of saw my mother as larger than life and somewhat timeless, so to speak, thinking she would live forever. I wasn't working at the time, so things were financially tough, but I managed to buy a ticket and head to Jamaica for the funeral

I won't go into my disappointment surrounding the funeral, but I will say that my brothers and sister were divided in every way, and this really had an effect on me, as I was used to seeing us all in unity. Anyway, my friend, Anne, helped me out financially while I was there, and I was able to do the things I needed to do independently. For that, I thank her with all of my heart.

Throughout all this, I didn't get teary until one day after returning from Jamaica. I was at work in my office — I had gotten a job as a traffic marshal — when all of a sudden and without warning, I started to cry. I tried to stop, but the tears just kept coming, so I let them flow. I missed my moms. If she were here now, I would thank her for her never-ending love and support. Thanks moms!

In 2017, some months after my moms had died, I was sitting in my one room in Lordship Lane, London, I had just come back from work, and I was hungry and tired, but I decided to unwind, so I scrolled through Facebook. As I was looking at the many faces, this particular one jumped out at me. It said her name was Andrene. I knew the name, but I couldn't make out the face as it had been a really long time since I'd seen her back home in Jamaica. I made a friend request, and we met up in Kentish Town and had lunch on her break.

We talked about everything and everyone we knew growing up. The very first school I had gone to, infant school, was run by a teacher called Miss Clariss, and we were in the same class. After that, we went to primary school, and we were in the same class again. I knew I'd known her after seeing her face on Facebook.

We had many dates after that, and after a while, we decided to live together at her place. We lived together for years, but sadly, the relationship ended. I would like to thank Andrene and her sister for the care, kindness, and love they showed me at that point in my life's story.

Here and Now

"

It is easier to build strong children than to repair broken men.
~ *Frederick Douglas*

"

IN 2019, I MET A wonderful woman. I used to work near where she lived, and I would say 'hi' to her whenever she passed by. She seemed kind of reserved, but I liked the way she carried herself. She had dreadlocks, for a start, which made me even more curious. She looked like a conscientious Black sister. One day, I saw her, and I crossed the road to talk to her. We spoke for a while before I asked for her number, which I didn't expect to get as women in England are so much more reserved than in the USA, but to my surprise, she gave me her card. I said I would call her on the weekend.

When she walked away, I looked at her card, and lo and behold, it was a business card that said she was a counsellor with expertise in trauma and recovery. That threw me a bit. I thought that maybe she was some kind of shrink that would try to analyse me at every turn, and by then, I'd had my share of being analysed. Eventually, I called her and suggested meeting up at Costa for a coffee. Whilst there, she told me about her writing a book, and I was so impressed and encouraged as I also wanted to write my own book but had never made a move. She taught me about book writing and encouraged me to write this book, and I thank her eternally.

At this present time, I am using my time to write this book, and I have the idea of a collection of short stories for a second book, but that's another story. These days, I try to live life to my potential and walk my talk. It has been a long, hard road, and I'm still jumping the hurdles in this rat race called life. I just want to end by saying that no one ever moves forward from standing still. Reach for your goals and aspirations and grab them with both hands. It's never the situation in which you find yourself; it's about what you are made of. It's about that something inside so strong that knows that we can make it if we work at it.

I would like to take this time to say that in writing this book, I am in no way glorifying crime and violence. I just wanted to take some time to share some of my life's experiences and in so doing, hopefully, enlighten or uplift someone in some way. I wanted to share that when a child is born into poverty-stricken, oppressive environments, childhood becomes a **Hood,** having a negative impact on children's chances in life, making the community—in this case, African, Caribbean, Black-British, and Black-American—stuck in a past filled with trauma for longer than young people are supposed to. Nas, a rapper, songwriter, and entrepreneur, raps about this on his track and album, *2nd Childhood*. What I call, **Message Music.**

I also want to say that as a group, Black people are bigger and better than what the system's statistics dictate. There is a saying that we are what we eat, meaning that whatever we put into ourselves, whatever we consume, is what we get out; I survived. This should not be good news. This is how it is supposed to be—more often—happening. I did not survive because of 'luck.' I sowed some bad seeds, but I mostly sowed some good ones that came back to find and bless me at key points in my life. I also came from a long line of progressive, intelligent, pioneering ancestors and relatives upon whose backs I stand. I also made it a point to learn from my experiences and not to bullshit myself. I was always able to stay within the confines of reality, live there, and use myself and my life as an example, which I now take to new levels in this book.

As a people, we are made of greater things and made for greater things. It is our mothers and fathers who are the founding mothers and fathers of civilisation and humankind. Know thyself, rise up and genius up. At this time of writing this book in 2022, having come out of COVID -19 and recovering from the murder of George Floyd, there is an enlightenment taking place. More and more good folks are waking up; more and more historical lies are coming into an undeniable light. Humankind is being dragged to human-up. At this time, we all have our parts to play, and must play.

This book is important for all of the above reasons but also because it is about an era and time that has received little reckoning or recognition, as is the case with all that was going on politically at the time. That time was when crack and cocaine were pushed onto the Black communities in the USA, Jamaica, and the UK, by governments wanting to fund a war in Nicaragua, which hastened the already struggling Black community's demise and Black-on-Black crime rocketed sky high. These communities are still coming back from that, and this genocide still very much continues today in the UK, JA, (Jamaica) and the USA. But time is a-changing, like I said. About time. We are all doing time; let's do time well.

Maurice Lennon August 2022

About Maurice Lennon

MAURICE LENNON IS A 60-year-old father of three children and grandfather of two grandchildren. He works as a traffic marshall in the construction industry. When he is not doing that, you may find him in the gym as he is a great lover of sports and athletics. He also loves to read books that are culturally, spiritually, and mentally uplifting and informing.

Maurice first discovered a love for the English language and literature in early childhood. After hearing about his life, a number of key individuals have said that he should write his own story.

Maurice is a man of stories, and he loves to share them in oral and written form. He is a student of life and likes to observe and learn from it. He is excited to be doing so in the writing of his first book and life story, **From ChildHOOD to Man.** He also plans to turn his attention to short stories: stories with messages that invite the reader to learn from life by listening to other stories where people, like Maurice, have triumphed over adversity, beating the statistics. Self-knowledge and self-confidence is everything, as the late great Marcus Garvey said:

'If you haven't confidence in self, you are twice defeated in the race of life. With confidence, you have won even before you have started.'

Acknowledgements

THANKS TO CONSCIOUS DREAMS Publishing for accepting my dream and helping me make it reality. Your support and help have been real. Daniella and her team provide this service with such grace, skill and know-how. They made the process very comfortable and encouraging, which is what I needed as a first-time author. Thank you!

Transforming diverse writers
into successful published authors

 www.consciousdreamspublishing.com

 authors@consciousdreamspublishing.com

Let's connect

Lightning Source UK Ltd.
Milton Keynes UK
UKHW020200240223
417572UK00014B/682

9 781915 522177